THE HEART CRIES OUT

A PARTICIPATORY BIBLE STUDY ON SELECTED PSALMS

Participatory Study Series
#17

DAVID MOFFETT-MOORE

Cover Design: Henry Neufeld
Cover Image: Adobe Sotck #144067714

ISBN: 978-1-63199-732-7
eISBN: 978-1-63199-733-4

LCCN:

Energion Publications
PO Box 841
Gonzalez, FL 32560
http://energion.com
pubs@energion.com

For my Mother, Ruth, in Memoriam

ACKNOWLEDGMENTS

Every book is a compilation of recommendations, suggestions, and encouragements for which a single author or small group of authors is accredited. This is certainly true for this volume on the Psalms. I should acknowledge all my Sunday School and Vacation Bible School teachers who force-fed me on the words of the Psalms so that I might grow to know the spirit of them as well. My mother, whose deep personal faith fed and formed the faith of her five children. She felt a call to ministry when women were discouraged from it, worked as a layperson in the church, married my father a minister, since she couldn't become one, heard the bishop tell his male pastors to keep their wives out of their parishes, so we five kids became her congregation. Henry and Jody Neufeld of Energion who restored my energy and imagination when I waned. Chris Eyre, also of Energion, whose critical eye made for a better offering. My good friends and colleagues, Rev. Kyle Tade and the Rev. Steven Mullin, honorably retired, who gave so freely of their time, talent and training so that this text might actually be finished. My wonderful wife, Becki, whose patience is beyond numbering and whose support is as gentle as it is steadfast. And to all the members of all the churches I have been privileged to serve, who have listened to the cry of my heart in so many sermons and lessons. God is patient and passionate, longing to hear from us, God's holy children, and we are like E.T. the Extra-Terrestrial, anxious to phone home!

TABLE OF CONTENTS

ON THE PSALMS

This is not a scholarly work. It is not an intellectual examination of the ancient writings of the Hebrew Bible. It is not a study of theology or even poetry. The Psalms have long been a part of the devotion of the Christian church and the individual Christian since the time of the crucifixion itself. This is such a devotional expression. It is an expression of adoration and admiration, of love for the text and tone of this book, this canon of Scripture. If I accomplish my goal in writing this, you will be inspired to read the Psalms for yourself. Not to study them, but to enjoy them, to let them into your heart rather than your head, to let them become spiritual seeds for your subconscious soul, to listen to them and allow them to resonate in your daily life.

When I have wanted to turn myself over to the compassionate care of a loving God, when I've had that hungering in the soul that words cannot describe, when I have been filled with emptiness and burdened with doubt and despair, when I've had nothing left to give, I can go to the Psalms. The Psalms give me the words I cannot find, they speak for me when I cannot speak for myself. They ask the questions I fear to speak. They share the feelings I refuse to acknowledge. They keep me honest and hold me accountable when I want neither. It is no wonder they are so dearly loved, not only by the faithful of the ages, but by Jesus himself. He shares widely from the Old Testament and especially from the book of Psalms, more than from any other book in the Old Testament.

May this study not only speak to your heart, but open your heart, perhaps even break your heart, before that divine presence that we choose to call God.

This study guide consists of three sections:
1. Introductory information
2. Study sheets
3. Appendices

As you prepare to enter this process of biblical study, it involves several steps reflecting the principles of *lectio divina*. You may have other ideas or even a completely different method, and that is fine, but it will still help if you understand the starting point.

You should also have some kind of guideline for how you will approach your study. That guide is going to suggest a process of study, which I'll repeat briefly here:

1. Preparation, including materials, prayer, and opening your mind
2. Overview
3. Background
4. The inner cycle (or central loop): Meditate, Question, Research, Compare
5. Sharing

This is a study process and it says very little about what you might do at each step of the process. It is, however, built on the principles of *lectio divina*, or "holy reading." Let's summarize those principles first and then look at the steps and see how they will help you apply these same principles to your study.

Holy Reading: A Model for Bible Study

Lectio divina, which means holy reading, is an ancient practice of studying scripture. There are many ways to practice *lectio divina*. It has been done in many ways since Origen described it around 220 CE. The great monastic traditions of the church further developed it into distinct phases and practices. The basic principle is that reading and studying the Bible should be remarkably different than reading the morning paper or studying Shakespeare. The Bible is a sacred text; it is a Living Word. It should not be studied as if it were a collection of dead pages from history.

When the two men were walking down the Road to Emmaus, they met the risen Christ, but did not recognize him (Luke 24). As they were walking down the road, Jesus interpreted to them the biblical story. Only later, as they were breaking bread, did they realize that Christ was with them the entire time.

Lectio Divina is a practice that, through the power of the Holy Spirit, invites the risen Christ to interpret scripture to us anew. It is a prayerful reading of scripture that expects God to speak once again through this Holy Word. Prayer should influence the way you study the Bible, and studying the Bible should influence the way you pray. In *lectio divina*, it is impossible to tell when you are studying and when you are praying, as there is no difference.

This practice is usually applied to small passages of scripture for an extended period of time. However, in this study *lectio divina* is used as a strategy to study an entire book of the Bible. This is somewhat challenging because the scripture text is so large, but the prayerful approach is still crucial to Christian study of the scripture. In these lessons, the ancient practice of lectio is blended with modern study methods that consider the historical, cultural, and literary contexts.

The historical methods are important to us because they help connect us to people of a different time and place who experienced the same God that we do, learned from the same texts, and were led by the same Spirit. In this context we do not study history for its own sake; we study history so that we might meet those who wrote the texts and those who have studied the passages before us.

The lessons in this guide are designed around the four movements of *lectio divina* established by Guigo II, a 12th-century Carthusian monk, in a book called The Monk's Ladder. He organized the practice around four rungs that help us draw closer to God through reading the Bible.

Reading (*lectio*): The first rung of the ladder is reading. Believe it or not, this is the step most often skipped or diminished. It is important to do the Bible reading for each lesson to get the most out of it. Ideally, it should be read several times so that you can become familiar with the language and themes of the text. This book is a guide to help you study the biblical text. It is a supplement to the text itself, and the text of scripture should be the primary focus in your study. The steps of the participatory study method emphasize different ways of reading to help the text become part of you as you study.

Meditating (*meditatio*): The next step is to prayerfully meditate on the text. Dig deep into it. Study the words. Break it down into pieces. In this study, this is where most of the background information is located. Look up words to find their meaning. Notice if there are any words or actions that the Holy Spirit may be leading you to examine further.

Praying (*oratio*): Third, we learn to pray the text. Use what you have learned from the scripture to formulate a prayer. It may be helpful to write it down. (There are note pages at the end of each chapter.) At the end of each lesson is a prayerful exercise that expounds on one of the themes from the text. Feel free to add your own prayers. This is where the text really becomes alive to us.

In the method used for this study guide, prayer is not seen as simply one part of the study; prayer permeates your study. You start with prayer and listening so that you will hear what God has to say through the text. Then you end by turning what you have heard from God back into prayer. The prayer never ceases!

Contemplating (*contemplatio*): The last step is the most difficult and rewarding. You have **read** the text, **studied** the text, **and prayed** the text. Now it is time to **be** the text. Let it seep into your being. Be still and listen. Make sure you leave some time after the prayer for silence and reflection. It is said that Dan Rather once interviewed Mother Theresa about her prayer life. Rather asked her, "What do you say to God when you pray?" Her answer was simple; "I don't say anything; I just listen." After that he asked, "Well, what does Jesus say to you?" And Mother Theresa answered, "Oh, He doesn't say anything, either. He just listens." Listening is what is important. You may not always feel anything, but God is there. Another facet of contemplation is to learn to *do* the text. We cannot be just hearers of the word; we must also be doers of the word. Let the scripture change the way you live your life.

St. John of the Cross said, "Seek in reading and you will find in meditation; knock in prayer and it will be opened to you in contemplation."

Applying the Principles in Participatory Study

Preparation

As you begin the study, preparation will involve getting the materials you want to use, then prayer to begin each session of study. Part of this introductory time will be making decisions about the time and resources you can devote to this study. This is also your time of prayer. Before you begin to read, you need to pray. Then you need to listen. You come to the text because God calls you to it.

Overview

Getting the overview is accomplished by reading through the Psalms. They were not written to be read as a unit but as separate compositions. Still, it is good to become familiar with the texts, I suggest using a translation that you might not normally use so that the words might be fresh for you. This is part of *lectio* but only part. You will learn to read in other ways in different phases of your study. Once you have read the Psalms through, read one or two of the following

1. The entry on the Psalms in a Bible handbook
2. The entry on the Psalms in a Bible dictionary

3. The introductory note on the Psalms in a study Bible, if you're using one.

4. The introductory section of a good commentary on the Psalms.

Here is where we introduce historical elements into your study. Don't imagine that God cannot talk to you through this text because you are so far separated from the people who wrote it. They were people like you who had hopes, dreams, gifts, and failings. Study the background to help you connect to them. Christianity is a community that extends not only in space right now but in time.

The Central Loop

For this overview, your central loop, as I call it, is your whole study of the book. Keep in mind that no element of your study is something you do just once and then forget about it. Prayer is continuous. There are multiple ways of reading, questioning, studying, and sharing.

For this study, I have divided this study of the Psalms into five units. Additionally, we begin with an introductory session and conclude with a summary session. The Psalms themselves consist of five books, in imitation of the five books of Moses. These miniature psalters are of widely varying lengths. Each week we will read approximately the same length from this text and from the Psalms, though there will be some variation in lengths. Hopefully, this will make your study more manageable.

In preparing this text I considered writing different chapters for each of the different types of Psalms: liturgical, thanksgiving, personal and corporate laments, enthronement, imprecatory, wisdom, etc. It occurred to me that this is not how we read the Psalms. We don't typically pick and choose our way through the Psalter, selecting one particular style or theme of psalm to read. We open the Bible to the Psalms and read and pray our way through. The angel said to St. Augustine, "Take and read!" We take and read, and find ourselves opened up by the scripture as we open it up before us. We take and read and find ourselves to be read.

My sister Susan's first husband was a brittle asthmatic who had tremendous respiratory problems late in his life. Frequently he had difficulty breathing, let alone sleeping through the night. Susan would sit on the floor beside him in bed, take her Bible in hand, open it to the Psalms, and beginning reading and praying and crying her way through them. That is how we read the Psalms! We will simply read through the psalms with chapters of approximately the same length.

My hope is that we can catch the spirit at work through the Psalms. These are not rules and regulations; the Psalms are not used to establish church doctrine. It is the prayer book and hymnal of the faith; collectively they are an act of worship more than a lecture to study.

This study is most closely related to *meditatio*, but the implementation of *meditatio* extends into the next section where you question the text in a directed way. Don't concentrate on the boundaries between one activity and the next. They are all related!

With each unit, there will be an opportunity to try to think of new questions one might ask for further study. Generating new questions helps keep us from getting stale. Not only do I not have all the answers; I don't even have all the questions! Think of a question primarily as a way to prepare your mind to hear the text. When we listen or read, we often hear what we expect to hear. If I'm listening to the radio for the weather, I may miss a major discussion of politics. You can miss what God is saying to you through a Bible writer because you are looking for something else. Questioning is an important part of *meditatio*, but it also relates closely to *oratio*— take your questions to God in prayer.

Finally, find something to share. Remember that sharing can be in the form of a question. For example, one might ask others how they understand a particular word, such as "incarnation," "poverty," or "atonement." Take notes on their answers, and bring that information back to your study. Then ask yourself what your neighbors will hear when you make particular statements, such as "I must be bold for Jesus!" or "Jesus is the only way to receive atonement." Do those statements mean something to them? Do they mean the same thing to them as they do to you?

This is part of *contemplatio*, as you try to be and do the text. We often think of sharing primarily as telling someone things that we have learned. But if what you learned is that God loves prisoners, for example, you might find that the best way of sharing that lesson is to become active in prison ministry. Sharing demonstrates that you don't believe the text is your private possession. It is God's gift to the Christian community.

Resources

The following resources are referenced regularly in the text. Additional resources are listed in the Appendix. In a small group, it is a good idea to have different members of the group bring different reference works. For individual study, use a selection:

1. Study Bibles. There are a considerable number of study Bibles available. Some take a more scholarly approach, while others are devotional. In selecting a study bible, it is best to begin by selecting a specific translation and then find a study bible that is based upon that text. The New International Version is very popular and there are a large number of study bibles related to it. While the NIV emerged from evangelical Protestantism, most mainline Protestant churches use the New Revised Standard Version. If your choice is the NRSV (as is true for me) then the leading options are: *The New Oxford Annotated Bible, New Interpreter's Study Bible, The Harper-Collins Study Bible*, and *The Access Bible*. Again, these are not the only translations or study bibles available for consultation, especially since the ones mentioned are based on the New Revised Standard Version. A note on study bibles in general—one should be careful to separate in one's mind the text from the commentary. It is easy to confuse them since the two are placed together.

It is, of course, always good to look at resources from a variety of perspectives, and thus resources beyond one's study bible should be consulted. Look at materials you are likely to disagree with to stimulate your thinking.

2. Concordances. You may decide to consult either English language concordances or those that include material on the original languages. If you get a concordance, find one that matches the Bible version you use. Besides print versions there are several free online sites that are helpful, including The Bible Gateway (multiple translations) and the Oremus Bible Browser (NRSV).

3. Bible Dictionaries. The information in a good bible dictionary overlaps what is found in many study Bibles and Bible handbooks, but they can be very useful for general study of topics being considered. It is important that if purchasing a bible dictionary to get an up-to-date one. See the resource list for suggestions.

4. Bible Handbooks. The information found in a Bible handbook will be similar to what is found in many study Bibles, only it will lack the biblical text.

5. Bible Commentaries. These resources offer more detailed exegetical explanations and interpretation of the actual text. They range from one-volume to multiple volumes. In purchasing commentaries, it is best to stay away from sets such as *Matthew Henry* or *Jameson, Fawcett, and Brown*. These were written several centuries ago and lack the kinds of historical and linguistic information you will need for deeper study. They can have some devotional value, but they can be found online.

When it comes to comparing passages, you will find your study Bible, concordance, and any Bible with reference notes to be very useful. Remember, however, that even the cross-references are just someone's opinion of how one passage is related to another. You don't have to agree. Look at the passages yourself, and ask not just whether they are related, but *how* they are related.

Remember to keep an open mind and a receptive heart while studying the Bible. Study prayerfully. Meditate on what you read.

Try to place yourself in the audience of people who might have first heard this book read to them aloud in a small house church.

WELCOME

"Know that it is God who has made us, not we ourselves. We are God's people, the sheep of God's pasture. Enter the gates with thanksgiving and the courts with praise. Give thanks to God! Psalm 100:3-4

Psalms: Prayers and Poems

The book of Psalms is the prayer book and the hymnal of the Bible. It is the book that Jesus quoted from most frequently. If it is Jesus' favorite book, his followers should be familiar with it as well. The early Christian monks memorized the Psalms in their entirety and prayed through the Psalms every week. During the Reformation, the Psalms were the source for the hymnody of the Protestant Reformation. Today the Psalms continue to inspire and give voice to our devotional lives. Throughout history, the Psalms have challenged us to be more open in our relationship with God, more honest in our prayers, more intimate in our faith experiences. Psalms draw us inward, drive us forward, and compel us upward.

In Jesus time, the Psalms were well known, regarded, and loved, but not universally considered Scripture and a source for doctrine, any more than we might consider our hymnals, our prayer books, our devotionals to be a source for church doctrine, as much as they may inspire us. Our hearts are warmed and our spirits fed as much by our favorite hymns and songs as by any reading of Scripture. They inspire us, encourage us, nurture and sustain us, but they are not Scripture. The Sadducees only accepted the five books of Moses as sacred Scripture. The Pharisees added in the books of history and of the prophets. Jesus, of course, is clearly in the line of succession of the great prophets of ancient Israel. While the Psalms were not regarded as Scripture, they were part of every synagogue and temple service and easily on the tongue of every practicing Jew.

The Psalms confess and complain like an impassioned lover in Psalm 42, "As the deer longs for flowing streams my soul longs for you, O God, my soul thirsts for You, for the living God. When shall I come and behold the face of my God? My tears have been my food day and night, while others say 'Where is your God?'" Psalm 62, "For God alone my soul waits, from God alone comes my salvation God alone is my rock and my salvation, my fortress; I shall never be shaken." From Psalm 102:4-7, "my heart is stricken, withered like grass. I am wasted, too wasted to eat my bread. My wailing and groaning wear me out. My bones cling to my skin. I am like a lonely owl in the wilderness, like a little owl in the wasteland. I lie awake; I'm like a lonely bird on the top of the house."

In the Psalms God is our passionate lover, our strong ally, our steadfast friend, our constant companion, our everlasting hope and our only refuge.

The historical roots of the Psalms go back to the Davidic dynasty. They show influence from all the nations and peoples surrounding ancient Israel. Many were composed in postexilic times and their final formation is as recent as a Maccabean period, 150–50 BCE. The book of Psalms is divided into five lesser books, mimicking the five books of Moses: Psalms 1-41, 42-72, 73-89, 90-106, 107-150, each one ending in a doxology. The popular belief was once David was their sole author, as Solomon was the sole author of Proverbs. We know this is not so. The prescript for Psalm 72 reads that this is the last Psalms of David, yet Psalms 86, 122, 138 and others are also attributed to him. In the ancient world, it was common practice to attribute authorship to famous people, so the Psalms attributed to David doubtless were not all composed by David, though some probably were.

There are also different types of Psalms included. Some are hymns or liturgies designed for public worship, many are laments either personal or corporate, and of course Psalms of Thanksgiving to balance out those laments. There are Royal Psalms and Psalms of enthronement for Royal use, liturgical psalms for use in public worship and wisdom and historical psalms for teaching. It was always an auspicious moment when a new King was crowned, especially if you were that new king! There are wisdom Psalms, such as Psalm 1.

And there are the imprecatory Psalms, the Psalms that appeal to God to go after our enemy. These Psalms challenge us to be more open and honest with God about our own feelings. The verses we leave out of Psalm 139, verses 19 through 21, "Oh that you would slay the wicked, God, that the bloodthirsty would depart. Those who speak evil and lift themselves against us for evil. Do I not hate those who hate you O Lord? Do I not loathe those who rise against you? I hate them with a perfect hatred; I count them as my own enemies." I wonder what a perfect hatred might look like. I wonder if our enemies are God's enemies, and God's enemies our enemies. I wonder what our perfect hatred might look like to the God whose name and nature is love. Yes, the Psalms give a voice to our own anger.

Psalm 137 begins as a beautiful mournful lament, "by the rivers of Babylon we collapsed and wept when we remembered you, O Zion. On the willow tree we hung up our lyres, for our captors required of us songs and our tormentors mirth." Yet the closing two verses reveal a different tone, "Oh Babylon you destroyer! Happy are they who pay you back for what you have done to us! Happy are those who take your little ones and dash their heads against the rocks!" Not words we expect to hear from the pulpit on Sunday morning, yet the sentiment that we all do feel from time to time. This is certainly a different beatitude. Blessing revenge and the slaughter of infants is hardly in keeping with blessing the poor in spirit, the merciful or the peacemakers.

Of the hundred and fifty Psalms, eighteen of them are imprecatory. That is better than ten percent. How much of our time do we spend being angry? Angry with road rage, frustrated in the checkout lane, upset by what we read on Facebook. Are we angry even 10% of the time? Do we carry that anger with us? Do we have a way to release that anger, to let go of the frustrations of life, to give up our hatreds and hassles and hurriedness, surrender it all to God, and simply let God be God?

The Psalms are perhaps more honest in their humanity than we are. We like to dress up for the divine, to pretend that we are more upright than we sometimes behave. The Psalms share the ache and pain of being human as well as the joys and victories.

The Psalms were written as songs and meant to be sung, meant to be part of public and private worship. They should be read as poetry, not theology. Let them be a source of devotion, not doctrine. A word that appears frequently in the Psalms and rarely anywhere else is "selah", a word of uncertain meaning. It appears 71 times in the Psalms and three times in the third chapter of Habakkuk, a prayer. Maybe it is a musical term, meaning "louder" or "softer", "faster" or slower." Maybe it is a call for the instruments to rest a while. Maybe it is a call for us to pause, to pay special attention. Maybe the entire Psalter is a call to prayer, to pay special attention to what God is doing in our lives. "Attend! Be mindful! Stay alert! Keep vigilant!" How many times did Jesus say this to his disciples? The source of all being, the Creator of the cosmos, the cause of it all, is entering our lives; don't miss it!

Question for reflection

Which are your favorite psalms? Which have you committed to memory?

Question for discussion

Are there psalms that have become part of your regular devotional life? How did this come to happen?

Question for Action

Take another look at those imprecatory psalms. When have you been this angry or upset? How can you integrate this into your devotional life?

Closing Prayer

God, you make us in your image and after your likeness. Our hearts cry out for your nearness. We ask that you would bless us through this time of study and fellowship, that we might draw nearer to you and to one another. Bless us with your spirit of grace and truth, of wisdom and understanding, we ask for your own name's sake. Amen.

PSALMS 1 - 23

"Lead me Lord, Lead me in your righteousness. Make your path plain before my face. For it is Thou, Lord, Thou Lord only, that cause me to dwell in safety." Psalm 5:8; 4:8

The way of blessedness

Psalm One encourages us in our spiritual pilgrimage. "Oh the bliss, O the blessed happiness, how enriched are those who do not follow the way of the wicked or the path of sinners or the seat of scoffers, but whose every delight, whose constant joy, is in the law of the Lord and on God's law they meditate both day and night." It is a wisdom Psalm written in the history of Israel to be the beginning of the book of Psalms. The beatitude is exaggerated and extravagant. "Oh, the extreme happiness, eternal joy, the bountiful blessedness of those who follow the way of blessedness." "Blessed are." This blessedness is not some promise of distant hope. The divine blessing is already here, already now. In the Beatitudes of Jesus in Matthew, the phrase "blessed are, theirs is," is a constant and consistent repetition. The blessedness of God is not some pie in the sky by and by, not just something we hope for but something we already have and possess.

The way of blessedness is contrasted with the way of the wicked, who are like the chaff discarded from the wheat, whose labors bear no fruit, and whose efforts no harvest. The blessed focus their lives on the divine; the wicked focus their lives on themselves. The contrast is between that which is timeless and that which is temporary.

Because God is love, the law of the Lord is an expression of that love. The law of the Lord is the way of life. It is not meant for us to beat ourselves over the head with, use as a weapon against one another, or as a barrier to the divine. The law of the Lord is an expression of the will of God, of God's yearning and longing and hoping for us as God's own children. An example of this might be seen in how we use the words of Jesus in John 14:6, usually translated "I am the way, the truth, and the life." I've seen this used as an exclusionary clause, a dividing line, a barrier rather than a bridge. This might just as accurately be translated, "I am the true and living way." Remember that the first followers of Jesus in the early decades of the first century were known as" followers of the Way," the Way being the person of Jesus Christ. The law of the Lord that we meditate upon both day and night is the longing, yearning, desiring of God for us to follow in this true and living way. It is a way that at the same time is both ancient and everlasting.

The path that God has prepared for us is radically personal, it involves the very soul and core of our being. It is also extremely practical; it is the way we are to live in our everyday lives. It is profoundly positive in its nature, its expectations, it's hope and desire for us all. And it is powerful, powerful enough to transform our lives and the life of all this world. The true and living way, the way that is ancient and everlasting, the way that God has prepared for us, is personal and practical and positive and powerful.

Our job, if you will, is to make heaven on earth, to make God's way our way. We work together for the common good and for the glory of God, to make the ancient and eternal way the way for us all here and now, to make Christ's prayer that God's will be done and God's kingdom come, on earth as in heaven, a living reality, to make God's law of love to be the way of the world. No small feat for us mere mortals!

For their part, the Psalms welcome us to a more open, honest, and intimate relationship with the divine presence in our everyday lives. The Psalms encourage us to be honest with our emotions, even our anger or hatred, that we might also be honest with our love, our hope, and our desire. The Psalms continue to be the book of prayer and praise, the book of hymn and song, the book that is honest to God and to ourselves, the book the challenges, comforts, nurtures and sustains us.

Thanks be to God!

Lead me, Lord

> "Lead me, Lord, lead me in your righteousness. Make
> your path plain before me, for it is thou, Lord, thou Lord only,
> that makes me dwell in safety." Psalm 5:8, 4:8

I grew up in United Methodist churches in small towns
throughout central Indiana. More than that, I grew up in the par-
sonages of these churches. It was a time when everyone went to
church on Sunday. You could not buy a gallon of gas or a gallon of
milk on Sunday morning, because no place was open. The choices
on Sunday morning were go to church or stay home. And if you
lived in the parsonage the choice was really just go to church.

Music played a central role in the worship service. The congregation always had a pipe organ, and there was always a choir to sing
the anthem and service music. We Methodists were quite proud
of our musical tradition. One of the co-founders of Methodism,
Charles Wesley, was a noted composer of church hymns, compos-
ing over 7000 hymns. Charles's son Samuel inherited a portion of
his father's talent. Samuel composed a sung response based on these
verses, Ps 5:8 and 4:8. I remember choirs singing this refrain several times a year, usually after the pastoral prayer. They convey the
near-constant attitude of the Psalms, of humility, openness, trust,
and absolute reliance on the steadfast love and abiding faithfulness
of an Almighty and all-loving God.

The world might be a scary place sometimes. We might fear
for our safety. We might be unsure of ourselves. We may not know
where we are going or what we are doing, or if it is what we are supposed to be doing and where we are supposed to be going. We face
unknown unknowns, we can't know all that we don't know. There
may be very little in our lives of which we may be certain, that we
may have confidence about. But one thing that we can know with
absolute certainty is the abiding presence of Almighty God.

I find myself repeating the words of these two joined versus even subconsciously. I mentally sing the refrain as easily as I draw breath, and sometimes is frequently. I will say it again, "lead me Lord, lead me in your righteousness. Make your path plain before my face. For it is thou, O Lord, thou Lord only, that cause me to dwell in safety."

How majestic is your name!

Psalm 8 celebrates God's creation. This short Psalm captures the essence of the theology of the entire Psalter. It expresses variance and understanding of God that is found throughout the Psalms. It was the scriptural cornerstone for my book on the theology of creation, *Creation in Contemporary Experience.* It celebrates both holy majesty and human dignity.

> "Oh Lord, our Lord, how majestic is your name in all creation! You set your glory above the heavens, yet out of the mouths of the youngest and weakest, you have founded a fortress against your foes, to silence the enemy and the avenger. When I gaze at your heavens, the creation of your imagination, the moon and stars you set in place, what are we that you are mindful of us? What are we that you should care for us? You made us little less than yourself, even crowned us with beauty and wisdom. You have placed us over the creation you have made, you've placed us over all things, all tamed animals and all wild beasts, the birds of the air, the fish of the sea, whatever passes along our paths. O Lord, our Lord, how wonderful your name in all creation!"

What a wonderful God, God is! God chooses to reveal God's self in and through the work of God's creation. Augustine and Aquinas both said that if we do not understand creation, we cannot understand the Creator. Creation is part of God's revelation of God's purpose and person to us all. God is wonderful and wondrous. Creation is majestic and mysterious, filled with diversity and divinity. We are God's children and a part of God's creation. A part of creation, not apart from God's creation. We are stewards of the sacred, responsible for our care of all creation. We are to till God's garden and tend God's flock. As stewards none of it is ours; all of it is God's, and God has entrusted to our care. We are accountable for that care. The purpose of an all creation is to reveal and celebrate the goodness and glory of God, to acknowledge and acclaim the blessedness of being alive. "O God, our God! How wonderful you are and how filled with wonder is all your creation! How great it is to be alive and aware, to experience this gift of life and to be even a small part of the wonder of your creation!"

Standing before God

Psalms 15 and 24 are both identified as Psalms of David. They speak of entering the sanctuary and ask the question "Who is worthy?" Of course, no one is worthy; we enter by the grace of God. God loves us because God loves us, God accepts us because God accepts us. This is simply the way it is. Yet there are expectations and encouragements.

> "God, who may live with you? Who may abide in your Holiness? Those who walk blamelessly, who do what is right, who speak the truth, who do not slander, who do no evil to their friends, nor take a reproach against their neighbors, who despise the wicked and honor the faithful, who stand by their oath even to their own harm, who are not money grabbers or bribe-takers." (Psalm 15)

> "Who shall climb God's holy hill? Who can stand in God's holy presence? Those who have clean hands and pure hearts, who do not do what is false or speak what is deceitful."(Psalm 24:3-4)

I don't know if there is any historical connection between these two Psalms. They are in relative proximity with each other, but that does not mean they are related to each other. However, I have always placed them together in my mind.

I suppose it is human nature to ask the question, "what must I do to be saved?" Even the rich young ruler wanted to know. It is an ongoing theme in church circles. I find it interesting to note that these two Psalms do not speak of what we believe, but rather how we behave. They do not speak of how we relate to God, but rather how we relate with one another. If we expect to get along with the divine, we had better find ways to get along with each other!

Be honest and civil in all our dealings with one another. Speak the truth and do what we already know to be right. Don't gossip! Don't take advantage of another person's misfortune, but rather assist them in their need. The latter half of verse four in Psalm 15 has long caught my eye. Stand by your word even to your own harm! Remain true even if it costs you. Avoid people who choose to live otherwise.

These are all pretty basic, common-sense rules and guidelines. It is surprising to have the entrance to eternity so simply described. It is important to note that the guidelines are all about how we live together in our communities and societies. It is not about believing in some special way, not about doctrines or church law or statements of faith, but even as Jesus said, "Love your neighbor as you love yourself. Love one another. No exceptions!" This is not only how we enter heaven, it is how we build a heaven on earth.

A holy sneeze

At the beginning of my ministry and the beginning of my love affair with the Psalms, Psalm 18 became one of my early favorites. It is a royal Psalm and a thanksgiving Psalm. It is identified as a Psalm of David, on the occasion of his escaping from King Saul. It is a Psalm that Hollywood could easily turn into a movie; it begs for special effects and computer graphics. It is a grand and glorious celebration of deliverance from a certain death. I enjoy reading it with all the drama I can muster.

"The cords of death attacked me; the torrents of damnation assaulted me; the ropes of hell trapped me tight; the snares of death confounded me. In my destruction, I cried out for God, for my God to help. From God's holy temple, God heard my voice, my cries reached God's ears. Then the earth reeled and rocked and roared. The foundations of the mountains trembled and quaked in fear for God was aroused. Smoke rose from God's nostrils, dividing a fire from God's mouth, glowing coals flamed forth from God's presence. God bowed down the heavens and God came to my aid. Thick darkness hid God. God Rode on angel's wings and flew; God came swiftly on the wings of the wind. God made darkness a covering, a canopy of thick clouds dark and threatening. Yet out of the brightness before God, there broke through the clouds stones of ice and coals of fire. God thundered in the heavens, the Most High spoke. God sent forth arrows of lightning. God exposed the floor of the sea and the foundation of the world, at God's rebuke, at the blast of the breath of God's nostrils." (Psalm 18:4-15)

I remember leading the youth group in a study of Psalm 18 and saying that these verses, ending with the phrase "at the blast of the breath of God's nostrils," described a sacred sneeze; this is the effect of God saying "Achoo!" I don't know that my Old Testament professor would agree with that assessment, but I still find it quite picturesque. The Psalm's experience and understanding of the divine is one of unlimited power, infinite wisdom, unassailable rule, and a profoundly intimate presence. The Psalm goes on to regale the virtues and attributes of the divine, of the psalmist's own innocence before God and absolute confidence in God's guidance, protection, and deliverance.

The Psalm ends with the blessings and abundance of God, saying "I will glorify God among all the nations, and sing praises to God's holy name. Great victory God has given us and shown steadfast love to all the anointed."

My God, Why?

Psalm 22 is another Psalm of David and a Psalm for deliverance from suffering. For us Christians, this psalm is most readily identified with the crucifixion of Jesus. It is filled with images that are readily identified with the passion of our Lord. It opens with Jesus' cry of abandonment on the cross, "My God, my God, why have you forsaken me?" It continues, "all who see me mock me, they make mouths and shake their heads at me, "he committed his cause to God, let God deliver him!" (v.7-8) "I am poured out, my bones are broken, my heart is wax, melting inside me. My mouth is dry as the dust of the earth, my tongue sticks to my jaw, I lay in the dust of death. My hands and feet are pierced, I can count all my bones. They cast lots for my clothing."(v.14-18) We see all these words fulfilled in the actions on and around the cross; it is as if an ancient and forgotten prophecy has come to terrible fulfillment.

Of course, it is always possible that the gospel writers used the words of Psalm 22 to describe the terrible awfulness of the crucifixion. Most Jews in Jesus' time lived in anticipation of the coming of the Messiah and the making of a new world. They expected the Messiah that would come in triumph. They expected the New World order would be established by divine will. They did not expect Isaiah's suffering servant or a sacrificial lamb. They did not see the Messiah in the words of Psalm 22.

I have heard many wonderful, moving Good Friday sermons on Jesus' cry of dereliction from the cross, "my God my God, why have you forsaken me?" I think there's more to the story.

When I say that I want to sing "The Old Rugged Cross," or "I Come to the Garden Alone," or "Amazing Grace," I mean that I want to sing the entire hymn, not just that phrase. When Jesus said, "my God, my God, why have you forsaken me?" He was not crying out in desperation to God who has already promised never to abandon or forsake us, not even in the entire collection of Psalms, which celebrate God's steadfast love and abiding faithfulness. Jesus was referring to the entire Psalm, the God who does not despise or abhor us, who does not hide from us or abandon us, but the God who rescues us and delivers us. The Psalm ends proclaiming, "all the ends of the earth will remember and turn to God; all the families and nations will worship God. For dominion belongs to God who rules over the nations, awake or asleep, alive or dead. Future generations will proclaim God's deliverance saying all that God has accomplished."(v. 24, 27-31) I look at Jesus' cry from the cross as a cry of affirmation and assurance, that even on the cross God does not abandon us or betray us. Even in the harshest of times, the worst of circumstances, even in the presence of death itself, God reigns!

Martin Luther King, Jr. said "the arc of history is long, yet it bends towards justice." I would say the arc of history is long, and it is bent at the hands of a loving and powerful God, whose love will ultimately triumph.

The Shepherd's Psalm

What new word can be said about the 23rd Psalm? It is nearly everyone's favorite psalm, even favorite scripture passage. Psalm 23 and the Lord's prayer are equally planted deep in every Christian's subconscious. We can recite these words without thinking. Nearly every funeral includes Psalm 23. We memorize these words in Sunday school or vacation Bible school. When I recite them, I may be looking at the New Revised Standard Version or Eugene Peterson's The Message, but the words which come out of my mouth are those of the King James version, the words I learned as a young boy. These are words that comfort everyone who reads them.

The 23rd Psalm epitomizes our ideal relationship with God. We want God to be our good Shepherd, guiding us through green pastures and calling us beside still waters. We want God to be with us as we go through that dark and lonely valley, even the shadow of death. Moses was a shepherd, tending the flock of his father-in-law Jethro, when he encountered the burning bush and heard the voice of God. Young David was a shepherd tending his father's flock when the prophet Samuel called him to be king of Israel and the slayer of Goliath. Rulers and leaders of Israel are challenged to be shepherds of their nation. Jesus is the Good Shepherd, laying down his life the sake of his sheep. The title "pastor" comes from the Latin word for shepherd. We want this Psalm to be our psalm.

I remember a sermon illustration but not its source. There once was a fancy cocktail party, and guests were asked to share their talents. Different people shared stories, told jokes, offered songs.

A renowned stage actor was asked to offer a dramatic recitation of Psalm 23, which he did, and received a warm and generous applause. A pastor who served at the local street mission was asked to offer his rendition. He recalled the words slowly, carefully, prayerfully. He paused as his voice cracked as he whispered the text. When he finished the room fell silent. The actor broke the silence, saying "I know the Psalm, but he knows the shepherd." We all know the words of the Psalm, but it's the presence of the shepherd that gives us comfort.

Question for Reflection

Consider your own experience of the Psalms. Has there been a time when you have turned to them for comfort or guidance? Reflect on that experience.

Question for Discussion

Psalm 1 and 15 talk about the way of blessedness and doing what is right. What is your reaction to their recommendations? Psalm 15:4 particularly praises "The one who swears to his own hurt and yet keeps his/her word." How is this attitude reflected in our society?

Question for Action

As you read through the psalms for next week, listen for a verse to stand out and speak to you. Take that verse or phrase with you from your devotional time. Committed it to memory and use it as a breath prayer through the active times of your day.

Closing Prayer

From holy sneeze to gentle shepherd, we experience your presence in our daily lives. You are a God is who is with us, always. Sometimes we may feel abandoned, but you never leave us desolate. Your steadfast love endures forever! May we grow in our awareness of your nearness, through this study and throughout our lives. Amen.

Psalm 24 – 51

"One thing have I asked of the Lord, this is what I seek:
that I may dwell in the house of the Lord all my life, to behold
God's beauty and seek God's wisdom!" Psalm 27:4

One thing I seek

Psalm 27 is identified as a Psalm of triumph and of confidence and a Psalm of David. It opens and closes with words that are quite familiar to most congregations, but in between is a verse that has been a mission statement and purpose statement for me throughout my ministry.

"God is my light and my salvation, whom should I fear? God is the stronghold of my life, of whom should I be afraid? . . . I believe that I shall see the goodness of God in the land of the living. Wait for the Lord, be strong! Let your heart take courage! Wait for the Lord." (Psalm 27:1, 13-14)

These are words of confidence and encouragement in the midst of trial and tribulation, words of affirmation in the midst of doubt and confusion. We can trust in God in any situation, we can have confidence in any circumstance. There is no need for doubt or fear, for second guesses or despair. God's presence is continual as it is intimate. The God who is above and beyond is also the God who is ever and always with us. But the words of the Psalm that most to speak to me come from verse four: "One thing have I asked of the Lord, this is what I seek: that I may dwell in the house of God all the days of my life, to behold the beauty of the Lord, to seek after God's holy wisdom."

This is another verse that has always been on my heart, spoken or unspoken. It describes my sense of call to pastoral ministry, it describes my intellectual pursuit for holy wisdom, it describes my joy in being in the house of God. As my retirement approached, there was a sense of emptiness and abandonment. My lifelong pursuit had been God's wisdom and my lifelong pleasure had been God's house. All of that was to be no more. All that I had been and all that I had given my life to was coming to an end. I was lost and confused, filled with a sense of hopelessness and confusion. The one thing I asked for and that I sought was to be no more. The quiet times when I sat in the pews and prayed for the people I loved and served. The holy moments when I knelt before the altar in an empty sanctuary, alone with God. Those fleeting moments of eternity, when in the midst of leaving public worship I felt the divine presence and would choke up or tear up with joy and gratitude. I still ache for the loss. I understand now why it is so difficult and painful for pastors to retire; it is a giving up of all that we love and long for, it is being and becoming less and less. The Psalms are filled with a celebration of the presence, the power and the love of God. This is certainly "gospel" if ever there was "good news."

In the movie *City Slickers*, about men going through midlife, there is a scene between Mitch Robbins, played by Billy Crystal, and Curly Washburn, played by Jack Palance. Mitch is looking for happiness and meaningfulness at a dude ranch. Curly is a cowhand, content with his lot in life. Mitch asks Curly what it takes to find happiness. Curly looks at him and holds out a finger, saying "One thing. Find your one thing." Contentedness does not consist in a large number of things, but finding the one thing that is the heart and core of our lives, finding that and being true to it.

"One thing have I asked of the Lord," and for a time this one thing was granted to me. For this I am eternally grateful. I praise God for all that God has shared with me, all I have been privileged to experience. I will not complain that my time has passed or that my tenure has ended. I will give glory for the days that I have had, the beauty I have seen, the wisdom I have gained. Thanks be to God!

Into God's hands

In Luke's Gospel, Jesus' final words on the cross are, "Into your hands I commit my spirit." This comes from Psalm 31 verse five, a Psalm that mixes praise with complaint. The psalmist has cast his lot with God, living on God's terms and following God's ways. Therefore, the psalmist also expects God's favor; if I choose you, then certainly you will choose me! Isn't that what we expect?

I remember reading years ago Rabbi Kushner's book on Job, *When Bad Things Happen to Good People.*[1] We are not disturbed when good things happen to good people or when bad things happen to bad people. We will credit it to God's good grace when good things happen to bad people. But it is against our sense of fairness for bad things to happen to good people, yet they most certainly do!

There is no promise from God of divine protection as a consequence of our faithful intentions. We all know good people who have been pillars of the faith and ideal role models who have suffered, even severely, with perhaps some strength from their faith, but no protection. Psalm 31 begins "God, I have taken my refuge in you, let me never be ashamed!" But God makes no such deal. Jesus may quote verse five from the cross, "into your hands I commit my spirit," but he dies anyway.

I am reminded of the closing verses of the prophet Habakkuk, "though the fig tree should not blossom, there be no fruit on the vines, the yield of the olive fail, the fields produce no harvest, the flock be cut off from the fold, there be no cattle in the stalls, yet I will praise the Lord, I will rejoice in God my salvation. God is my strength, God makes my feet like the deer's, and causes me to dance on the heights." (Habakkuk. 3:17-19) Though all I may see be a slow, painful, certain death, yet I will praise God.

Jesus warns us that God causes the sun to shine and the rain to fall on good and bad alike. We ought not be surprised when that happens. This is not a "you wash my back and I'll wash yours" situation. God makes no deals!

---

1   Harold Kushner, *When Bad Things Happen to Good People*: Random House 1981

We are all going to die. We rarely get to choose how or when. We only get to choose how we live, not how we die. We choose what our lives stand for, what we live for. Mindful of this fact, the Psalm ends with this encouragement, "love the Lord! Be strong, take courage, hope in God."

Our Divine Lover

"As the deer pants for water, so my soul pants for you, O God! My soul thirsts for you, the living God!" (Psalm 42:1-2)

The Bible has many descriptions for the divine. We are probably most familiar with the persons of the Trinity, whether the traditional Father, Son, and Holy Spirit or more inclusive Creator, Redeemer and Sustainer or Source of all Being, Ever speaking Word and Life-giving Spirit. We can easily add Lord, master, shepherd, friend, even brother. We are less familiar and less comfortable with thinking of God as our Divine lover, yet it is certainly an image found in Scripture. The Song of Songs reads like a wedding feast between the human soul and the divine lover. It was the most popular source for spiritual commentaries through the Middle Ages and served as inspiration for John of the Cross's *Dark Night of the Soul.* I like to think of God loving us with a passionate love. Not just a love that holds us in high esteem or great regard, but a love that motivates and empowers, a love that is passionate.

I have preached that God loves us the way a 13-year-old loves, with the love that drives and distracts, a love that keeps us from eating or sleeping. This is a love worth dying for! In my younger days, my pilgrimage was more of a compulsion, perhaps even an addiction. I hungered and thirsted for the experience of the divine. I skipped meals and missed sleep. I wanted God so much that I ached. I am older now and my emotions more mellow, but I confess to missing that passion, that hungering and thirsting of the soul that only God can satisfy.

The Beatitudes say "Blessed are those who hunger and thirst for righteousness, for they shall be satisfied." Luke's version does not spiritualize this hunger, saying, "Blessed are you who hunger now, you will be filled." Few of us know what real hunger is, though studies indicate one child in six suffers from food insecurity. We might skip a meal to drop a pound or two, but few of us suffer from starvation. What is it like to be hungry, and not be able to satisfy that hunger?

"My soul pants for God, my spirit thirsts for the only true God." How desperately do we seek the divine? In *Addiction and Grace*,[2] spiritual director and psychologist Gerald May argues that the tendency to addiction is part of the human condition, and addiction is a human substitute for our longing for God. Of course, there is no substitute for the ultimate Real Thing! We long for divine meaning and connection, and try all manner of artificial replacements. We cannot substitute the penultimate for the truly ultimate.

There's a story of a Buddhist pilgrim happening upon a Buddhist monk. The pilgrim confesses an anxiety to find God and described a desperate search. The monk invites the pilgrim to enter a river together. Doing so, the monk forces the pilgrim's head underwater, holding it there through all the thrashing about. Finally the monk pulls the pilgrim's head out of the water. The monk asks the pilgrim, "What did you want, under the water?" "Air!" was the quick reply. "How desperately did you want it?" "I would die without it!" The monk then promised, "When you seek God as you would seek air, then you will find God!"

A Mighty Fortress

Martin Luther was a man searching desperately for God, as student, as monk and priest, and as professor. He sought the assurance of faith, the confidence of God's grace in his life. He pored through the scriptures, embarked on pilgrimages, and exhausted his confessors. In the end, his desire for the divine broke the church in two. He loved his church, but he refused to recant, "Here I stand!

---

2   Gerald G. May, *Addiction and Grace: Love and Spirituality in the Healing of Addiction*, Harper One, 2006

God help me, I can do no other." And the Protestant Reformation was born.

The church and all Europe broke in two, there were riots in the streets and mobs in the fields, churches were desecrated and sacred relics destroyed. Thirty years of war and bloodshed ensued; it was a rough birthing! In all this, Martin Luther wrote "A Mighty Fortress Is Our God,'" inspired by the words of Psalm 46:

>God is our refuge and our strength, a very present help in our trouble.

>We will not fear, though the earth shake and mountains fall,

>Though waters rage and roar and mountains collapse.

>Cease your struggling and know God, exalted among all the people.

>The Lord of hosts is with us, the God of Jacob is our strength!" (46:1-3, 10-11)

God knows

I am guided in my faith by the words of Isaiah that Jesus quotes beginning his ministry in Luke 4:18-19 and in the parable of the Great Judgment in Matthew 25:31-46. These are calls for social justice, for equal opportunity, for right relations between people: feed the hungry, clothe the naked, welcome the stranger, care for the sick, free the oppressed. They are words and deeds that fall well into the guiding light of the prophetic religion of the prophets of Israel. They are also consistent with the words and warnings of Psalm 50:

>"Hear, Israel! I your God will testify against you!
>If I were hungry I would not tell you, for all the earth is mine.

>Shall I eat the flesh of bulls or drink the blood of goats?

Offer a sacrifice of thanksgiving and pay your vows to the Most High.
You hate discipline and toss off my warning,

You are glad with thieves and happy with adulterers,

You slander your own family and loosen your tongue with evil
Now hear this, all you who go your own way:

Only those whose way is true shall see the salvation of God!"
(Psalm 50: 7, 12-14, 17-20, 23)

The Sinner's Prayer

Psalm 51 is a sinner's Psalm, it is a penitent prayer for pardon. The scriptural notes say that it is a Psalm of David, when the prophet Nathan condemned him for his adultery with Bathsheba. It is also a part of the Ash Wednesday liturgy for the hard truth is that while we are the beloved children of a loving and generous God, we are also sinners who fall short of God's grace. It has been said that the line between heaven and hell, between good and evil, goes straight through every human heart.

Many are the times that I have prayed these words from this Psalm kneeling with my head bowed toward God's altar. Many is the time in my spiritual pilgrimage when I have wandered and gotten lost. With Paul in Romans chapter 7, I confess that I do not do the good that I should do, but the evil that I should not do. Many is the time that I have needed these words and this prayer. My hope is in verse 17, "The sacrifice acceptable to God is a broken spirit, a humble and contrite heart God will not refuse."

I have said in the past that everything I need to know about a person, I know as soon as they enter the church. First of all, I know they are sinners. All have sinned and fallen short of the grace of God, there are no exceptions, no, not one. But secondly, and more importantly, I know they want to do something about that first fact. People who are complacent about their faults or comfortable in their shortcomings do not come to church. Thirdly, and most important of all, I know that God loves them with an undeniable, unconditional, unquenchable divine and holy love. And it is my job to make sure this sinner stranger knows they are loved.

Question for Reflection

Look back over your life. Can you recall times when God seems to have been particularly present, guiding or protecting, comforting or renewing?

Question for Discussion

I close by saying there are three things I know about everybody before I even know their name. Does this ring true for you? Does it sound presumptuous or is it an accurate description of our human condition?

Question for Action

In light of Psalm 51, can you name someone you have wronged or injured in some way? How can you now make amends?

Closing Prayer

One thing we ask of you, God, that we may dwell in your holy presence all the days of our lives, to seek your wisdom and enjoy your beauty. We seek your face even in ways we do not know, yet you are nearer to us than we are to ourselves. We humble our hearts before you as we seek signs of your love and grace in our daily lives. Touch us and heal us, that our brokenness may be made whole again. Amen.

PSALMS 52 – 89

"God, you are my God! I seek you earnestly. My soul thirsts for you, my heart longs for you, my flesh faints for you!" Psalm 63:1

Practical atheism

Psalm 53 begins with the charge, "The fool says secretly 'There is no God!' They are all corrupt, committing abominations and injustice; no one has done good." This is a weighty charge indeed. Yet, it may also be accurate!

I have met few people who call themselves atheists, convinced there is no God. More who are agnostic, simply not sure or not convinced. I have more respect for the agnostics; who could be so vain as to be 100% sure one way or the other? Doubt is part of the human condition, even a necessary step on the way to belief. To doubt is to question, which is the first step toward a new and fuller understanding. But atheists are different. They are convinced there is no God. Of the few atheists I have met, though none of them would admit, the majority actually do believe there is a God and they are it: the supreme being in the universe, the most important of all creatures.

I have respect for agnostics and have had some scintillating conversations with some of them. Atheists are different. Too many of them consider themselves superior to anyone so weak as to rely on any given faith experience. The universe is vast beyond our knowing and we are infants in this voyage of creation. Who among us can dare claim to be absolutely convinced of anything? I've long held that the best way to start an intellectual discussion on nearly any topic is "I don't know, but it seems to me . . . "

Psalm 53 catches this attitude, the vanity of the intellectual atheists, and challenges them as corrupt fools. But there is another kind of atheist, much more common and much more dangerous. In addition to the intellectual or philosophical atheist is the practical atheist. This is the person who goes to worship on holy days, who verbally subscribes to a faith statement and even financially supports a house of worship, but their decisions and lifestyles are all in defiance of the faith they verbally proclaim. They talk the talk, but they do not walk the walk! I have found these practical atheists in every congregation I have served. God help me, there have been too many times when I have been among their number.

The words of verse three echo to my shame, "Everyone has turned aside; all are corrupt. There is no one who does what is right; no, not even one."

I don't know about you, dear reader, but I do know about me. I am easily persuaded to go after my own heart rather than follow in those blood-stained footprints of the Christ I claim to serve. My motives are seldom that pure. It is easy for me to do what I want when I want how I want and disguise it as following where Christ leads.

I will repeat again the ancient Pilgrim's Prayer, a prayer rooted in the desert fathers and mothers of the third and fourth centuries, a prayer that they would continually repeat to themselves throughout the day, as they busied themselves with their tasks and chores. Breathing in slowly and deeply, holding that breath, then exhaling slowly and completely. Feeling that emptiness, then repeated the prayer again:

"Lord Jesus Christ, son of God, have mercy on me, a sinner."
"Lord Jesus Christ, son of God, have mercy on me, a sinner."
"Lord Jesus Christ, son of God, have mercy on me, a sinner."

I cannot rely on my pretended righteousness. I cannot claim my good deeds as my defense. My words are only lip service and my motives can always be questioned. I can only fall upon the mercy of the God for whom I hope.

Waiting in silence

St. John of the Cross observed, "God's first language is silence." Thomas Keating added, "all else is a poor translation." I read of an ancient spiritual master, one of the desert fathers, whom the emperor came to visit. The emperor had heard so much about the father that he wanted to see for himself. All day the emperor waited. Finally, the monk implored the father to grant the emperor an audience. He replied, "If he doesn't understand my silence, he will never understand my words." Another desert father advised his followers, "Never speak unless your words improve upon the silence."

Psalm 62 confesses, "My soul waits in silence for God alone, from God is my salvation." (v. 1) My soul waits in silence for God alone, my hope is from God." (v. 5)

We are not a people who abide much silence! They say nature abhors a vacuum and we abhor the silence. We sit, walk and drive with our faces glued to our cell phones. We have radio and television on almost constantly, even just to keep us company. So we won't have to be alone in the silence! I have admitted that life seems better with a soundtrack (mine would be jazz or blues). Yet the sound of God's silence calls to us, even as the sirens of Odysseus.

God's first language is silence, all else but a poor translation. If we don't understand God's silence we will never understand God's words. Don't speak unless our words improve upon God's silence!

I do usually start my day with 20 minutes of centering prayer, sitting in silence, listening to God listening to me, as Mother Theresa described. Sitting in silence, listening to God's listening.

Years ago, when I was young and radical in my faith, I would spend my lunch hour sitting in silence, with the light of a single candle, breathing and listening. Being rather than doing. Waiting. An hour at a time.

On the Myers-Briggs Type Indicator I am INFJ: Introvert, not Extrovert; iNtuitive, not Sensing; Feeling, not Thinking; Judging, not Perceiving. Of the 16 different possibilities, this type accounts for 1% of the population yet 90% of the mystics. We are people who thrive on silence!

We each have our preferences for prayer and there are different approaches for different people, all of them good. I suggest that there are seven billion different paths to God, as there are seven billion people on this planet. God has a path for each of us. You might look at my book *Pathways to Prayer*. Silence is not of equal benefit to each of us, but some silence in every life and every day is a good thing. It is, after all, God's first choice to communicate.

In the silence, we can hear; in the waiting, we can receive: "Once has God spoken, twice have I heard: all power belongs to God; God's steadfast love endures forever"(vv. 11-12).

Thirsty souls

Have you ever stood in front of an open refrigerator, rummaging around for some left-over on the shelves, not sure what you are looking for yet sure that you can't find it? Who hasn't! Sometimes we are hungry and thirsty for what we cannot find because we are looking in the wrong places. Sometimes it isn't our stomachs that are hungry but our souls! I don't think it just a coincidence that our children are malnourished, our adults obese and our world suffering from a loss of spirituality. It is not just our stomachs that we need to feed!

Psalm 63 speaks powerfully and eloquently for our thirsty souls: "O God, you are my God. I search eagerly for you, my soul thirsts for you, my flesh longs for you, as a dry worn-out land, to see you revealed in glory. Your lovingkindness is better than life. In the shadow of your wings, I sing for joy." With Psalm 42, these two psalms give voice to the longing of spirit for Spirit, of creature for Creator.

Our hearts cry out, longing for God. We are as infants crying in the night to be comforted. We are as children fussing for food, not knowing what we want. We are as adolescents in the agony of raging hormones, exciting us with energies we cannot contain. We are adults, full but not fulfilled, busy yet bored, having it all and wanting none of it, thinking there must be something more. We seek, not knowing what we seek.

Augustine said we have a God-shaped hole within us and we can't be satisfied until it is filled. Teilhard de Chardin writes that we are not human beings having a spiritual experience but spiritual beings having a human experience.[3] The authors of the Human Genome Project say that we are designed in our DNA to believe in God, to want there to be some ultimate meaning to our existence. We are the temporary seeking the Eternal, the finite seeking Infinity.

To long for God is part of the human condition. This does not prove the existence of God, but it does prove that we want there to be a God.

We are an obese nation, too often feeding ourselves and our children junk food with little nutritional value: fast food, comfort food, convenience, and we are sedentary. We need to follow for simple words: "eat less, exercise more." And we need to admit that we have spiritual needs, spiritual hungers, that we are indeed spiritual beings, having a very human experience.

A simple prayer

I grew up not just "in the church" but in the parsonage! I would play in the yard between the church and the house, literally in the shadow of God's wings. The church building was as much part of my home as was the parsonage. If there was a program at the church, I was probably there. If I wanted to see my Dad, I would need to go to his office in the church, his "study." Doctors, lawyers, bankers, managers all have offices. Teachers have classrooms. Only pastors have studies.

Traditionally pastors have years of studying before they can begin their practices: four years of undergraduate studies, three years of graduate school, one or two internships, plus a full battery of personal, physical, psychological and theological exams to determine one's fitness for service. After this grueling gauntlet, then one can begin!

---

3   Attributed to Pierre Teilhard de Chardin in *The Joy of Kindness* (1993), by Robert J. Furey, p. 138

This makes us as a profession to be quite caught up in our words. We are not universally verbose, but we are people who make our living on our words. We are wordsmiths!

And yet sometimes simpler is better. Ancient Judaism had 636 laws to follow, but Jesus and the rabbis said "Love the Lord your God and your neighbor as yourself. This is the law and the prophets." Everything else was commentary. Augustine, the intellectual father of western Christianity, summarized it "Love God and do as you please." Because if we truly love God we would want to do what pleases God. Micah 6:8 summarizes prophetic religion, "What does the Lord require of us? Do justice, love mercy and walk humbly."

Sometimes simpler is better. The old "Kisss" formula: keep it short, sweet, and simple. Psalm 67 does just that; it is a simple, direct, honest, prayer and affirmation, thanking God for all God's goodness and calling the world to thank God. "God has blessed us, let the whole earth rejoice!"

When bad things happen

Rabbi Kushner's popular *When Bad Things Happen to Good People*[4] used as its scriptural base the book of Job, a good and righteous man who had many bad things happen to him. It could just as easily have used Psalm 73, which essentially expects God to do what we expect God to do: side with the good righteous people.

We have all experienced the reality that life is not always fair. Bad things happen to bad people, fine. That's as it should be. Good things can happen to good people; of course, they deserve it. Good things sometimes happen to bad people because God is gracious. But bad things should never happen to good people, especially to us! Then shall come to pass the saying: "Nobody likes me, everybody hates me, I'm going outside to eat worms!" We have our private little pity party.

Psalm 73 pleads with God to side with the righteous, especially to side with the author, and complains that the wicked seem to

---

4   Op. Cit.

flourish. They are getting away with it! But towards the end it has this wonderful passage:

> "Who do I have in heaven but you?
>
> There is nothing in this world I desire besides you.
>
> My body and spirit may fail,
>
> but God is the stronghold of my life
>
> and my strength forever" (Psalm 73:25-26).

It is the impassioned plea of a desperate lover, the cry of a lovelorn. Yes, there is good and bad, right and wrong. We humans are meaning-making animals, we want there to be order and rightness to our world. We bring morality into the equation. But I think God is a passionate God, God has yearning and desiring for us. God not only desires for us to do the right thing, God desires *us!* It is not enough for us to do right, we must give ourselves to God: hook, line, and sinker. Good things and bad things will continue to happen; the sun will shine and the rain will fall on good and evil alike. God longs for us to long for God, to hunger and thirst not only for righteousness but for God. God is our portion and our desiring!

Holding the world

We all probably grew up learning this spiritual at some time or another: "He's got the whole world in His hands" (with apologies for the sexist language). This is the declaration of Psalm 75, both in text and in tone. The psalm declares the power of God, the purpose of God, and the place of God, above and beneath all creation. It makes this declaration in confident, even child-like, trust, celebrating the goodness and the glory of God. God keeps creation from collapsing and God will judge the proud and the wicked.

The next time we feel like God has forgotten us, like the wicked are winning and the arrogant need a comeuppance, we can remember Psalm 75, halfway through the Psalter, and sing that little ditty about who it is that is holding the world, sustaining creation. and balancing the scales of justice.

Praying for peace

The Psalms repeatedly cry out for Jerusalem and the peace of Jerusalem. The city existed before the founding of the Hebrew nation or the conquest of the Promised Land. It was not renamed when David made it his capital. Its name might be translated as "The Place of God's Peace." As such, it has always represented the church, both as fellowship and facility. As a preacher's kid, I spent many long hours exploring and pretending within those sacred walls. Psalm 84 declares this affection for the place of worship. "How lovely is your dwelling place, O Lord of hosts!" Granted that the divine presence is everywhere and the sacred may be manifest at any time or place: golf courses, fishing streams, even the warm confines of one's bed-sheets, nonetheless we all have experienced some places as somehow more sacred. For the faithful, a week is simply not complete without a Sunday visit to a place of worship, "My soul longs for the courts of the Lord!"

In the death throes of the medieval church and birth pangs of the Reformation, Erasmus, the Dutch Humanist and philosopher, was prevailed upon to offer some plan or argument to keep the church whole, to avoid the split between Catholic and Protestant. He based his thesis on Psalm 84, this love poem for the place where God abides.

It's a wonderful world: Psalm 85

In the movie *Good Morning Vietnam*, there is a scene of American bombers destroying rice paddies, fields, and villages. It is a sunny, beautiful day, filled with destruction. In the midst of this violence, we hear the soundtrack of Louis Armstrong singing "It's a Wonderful World." We live in a world of danger and destruction, Daily facing risks of which we are ignorant. At the same time, it is a world filled with possibility and opportunity, a world of beauty and wonder.

The 85th Psalm reminds God that God has pardoned us, God has forgiven us our sin. It asks if God will be angry with us forever. It begs for God's steadfast love and salvation. But it ends with a wonderful description of holy embrace in the divine dance, "steadfast love and faithfulness will embrace, righteousness and peace will kiss, faithfulness will spring up from the ground and righteousness will beam down from the heavens. God is good and will provide for us and righteousness will be our path."

I remember a time when the church was going through some conflict and it was wearing on the staff. The wind and the waves of stormy personalities were tossing our good ship of faith to and fro. We came up with a catchphrase to remind us that even in the conflict and the chaos, God was constant. One of us would call out," God is good." And the other responded "all the time." Then we would reverse it: "all the time," and respond," God is good." In the nitty-gritty of our daily lives, steadfast love and faithfulness embrace and righteousness and peace will kiss, faithfulness will spring up and righteousness will beam down.

Julian of Norwich was a 14th-century mystic and theologian. She lived at the time when England was in Civil War and struck with the black plague. She was a single woman with no male to protect her. She was homeless and built a shelter outside Norwich Cathedral. She caught a fever and nearly died. During the fever, she received several visions. When she recovered, she recorded them in her revelations of divine love.[5] In this book, a lone woman, sick and homeless, surviving war and plague, declares, "all will be well, and all will be well, and all manner of things will be well."

Life is risk; there is conflict, confusion, and chaos. We are surrounded by danger and destruction. And in the midst of it all, God is good all the time, all the time God is good, and it is most certainly a wonderful world.

Psalm 85 ends with another one of my favorite verses:

---

5   Julian of Norwich, *Revelations of Divine Love,* multiple editions available.

"Steadfast love and abiding faithfulness will encounter,

Righteousness and peace will embrace.

Truthfulness will rise up from the earth

and righteousness look down from the sky.

The Lord God will give us what is good,

The whole world will yield a great harvest

Righteousness will go before and make a clear path to follow."   (Psalm 85: 10-13)

Question for Reflection

In spite of any personal maladies or the chaos our world may be in, can you say with Julian of Norwich, "All will be well"?

Question for Discussion

When was a time you felt the world was picking on you? How did that situation work out?

Question for Action

Identify an injustice in your community. Go out and do something about it!

Closing Prayer

The whole earth is alive with your glory, God! Your radiance shines in every corner of our lives if we but have eyes to see. In all our days we give you our praise. All our words are not enough to thank you,

yet words are sometimes all we have. So we give you our silent praise,
the joy of our grateful hearts. Thank you, God, for everything! Amen.

PSALMS 90 – 114

"Bless the Lord, O my soul! All that is in me, bless God's holy name! Forget none of God's benefits, who pardons your iniquities, who heals your diseases, who redeems your life from the pit, who crowns you with lovingkindness and compassion, who satisfies your years with goodness." Psalm 103:1-5

Eternal assurance: Psalms 90 and 91

David is by far the most common name attached to the psalms, fully half of the 150. Others associated with psalms include Asaph, the Korahites and Solomon. Moses gets one: the 90th. Moses is probably the second or third most important historical figure in Judaism, behind Abraham and possibly David. He is the Liberator, and as such recognized not only in Judaism but also Islam and Christianity. Psalm 90 speaks of God's timelessness and our transitoriness; as such, it is appropriately a prayer of Moses, the man of God. Moses faced Pharaoh, freed the Hebrews, led them through the wilderness to the promised land and made them into a nation, but he was not permitted to enter. Such is the way of God's promise and our frailty. It is the inspiration for Isaac Watts' hymn, "O God, Our Help in Ages Past."

Psalms 90 and 91 express thoughts relevant for the funeral of one who has lived long and well and much respected by their peers, one who has lived out the challenge of our baptism, to be a faithful witness of Jesus Christ. I've read selections from these psalms at several services, honoring a life well lived.

Between being a United Methodist pastor and a United Church of Christ pastor, I spent a decade or so in financial services, investments, and insurance. I figured if I wasn't in ministry, the reason for having a job was to make money and the best way to make money was with money. I would say the real product that

I was selling was trust: people wanted to know they could trust me with their money and their future.

Early on, my sales manager took me out for lunch. He wanted to know what motivated me. I was leading the office in sales, but he believed I could do better. So he asked me point blank, "David, what most motivates you? What do you most desire in this life? How can I help get that for you?" There was a long pause as I deliberated on that question. Finally I confessed, "I want to so live my life that when I die, the church will be packed and even the undertaker will be sad to see me go." He was taken aback, clearly not expecting that kind of an answer. He confessed he had no idea how to help me attain that. It was probably an early sign that, despite professional growth and success in the industry, I was destined to return to full-time ministry.

Get me to the church on time!

I grew up in a parsonage, meaning I grew up going to church. If the doors were open, we were there. If I wanted to see Dad, I went to his study. Every Sunday we went to church, every special service. The church almost became an extension of our house, another place to play.

Once I was doing just that: playing in the sanctuary. Dad came looking for me and I feared I was in trouble, so I hid - inside the access panel for the organ pipes. I squeezed in there, closed the door, and then realized how much trouble I'd be in if Dad found me there. Fortunately for my survival, he did not look there. Psalm 91's hiding place was in the shelter of the Most High, my hiding place had been the pipe organ.

I can think of a lot of times I have not been a good Christian. I can't remember a time I have not considered myself a Christian. Psalm 92 celebrates the sanctity of the Sabbath and the wonder of worship. Reading and reflecting on it is a good way to get started on a Sunday morning. In worship we are at play before the Lord, we delight in our God, we declare the value of God. "Worship" comes from the Anglo-Saxon "weorthscripe," meaning to declare the value, the worth, of an object. Worship is not a show we come to watch but an act we come to participate in, to stand in the presence of the Divine, to see God face to face. It is good to give thanks, to sing God's praises, and to show our love!

The Ultimate Avenger

I grew up reading Marvel comics with stories of superheroes: Spiderman, Daredevil, the Fantastic Four and the X-Men, Iron Man and the Mighty Thor and of course the Avengers. Today's youth don't have to read the comics, they can simply watch a world filled with superheroes on the movie screen. Marvel comics have revolutionized the movie business with the Marvel universe.

Because the God of the Bible is experienced quite personally, God is typically described as a person, a being, an entity. Our 21st century understanding of the Divine has evolved, so that we describe God as beingness itself rather than a being, as process more than person, as the whole of existence rather than a separate entity. Yet the ancient Biblical images still exist. See "A Contemporary Expression of the Eternal God" in my *Creation in Contemporary Experience.*

So in keeping with the Marvel Universe, Psalm 94 offers us a different and divine superhero: God, the ultimate Avenger!

God, who judges the earth, who metes out justice, who sees all that is hidden, who disciplines nations and decides among people, who knows our deepest secrets, who rules with righteousness, who alone is our strength and refuge, upon whom we can always rely with utmost confidence, who alone is ultimate and eternal. God is our force and foundation, so that we need have no fear. Not Thanos or the Red Skull, not Dr. Doom or Dr. Octopus, not Galactus or Ultron, Apocalypse or Archangel, but the Lord God Almighty shall prevail!

Joy to the world!

The history of Psalm 98's a good example of the use and influence the psalms have had on the church. The Psalm is an invitation to praise God. Basically, to praise God for being God, for God's righteousness, faithfulness, and lovingkindness. It invites all creation to join together in praising God.

Isaac Watts was a dissenting pastor and poet. He wrote two poems paraphrasing Psalm 98. The second poem became the hymn "Joy to the World." While based on Psalm 98 from the Jewish Scriptures, the lyrics of the hymn celebrate the second coming of Christ and his earthly rule, something the original author would never have conceived. The familiar tune was cobbled together from musical phrases from George Frederick Handel's *Messiah*. The American musicologist Lowell Mason matched the tune to the words and distributed them, making it one of the most widely published Christmas Carols in the United States.

I like to think that all creation is alive with the glory of God, that all creation constantly rejoices in God. Remember the tale of a mother in the Scottish isles, chastising her children for forgetting their prayers, cited in my book, *Life as Pilgrimage: A View from Celtic Spirituality,* "the sun shines in the sky for the love of God, the clouds floated by for the love of God, the trees bend in the wind for the love of God, the flowers bloom with the love of God, the waves dance and the fish swim for the love of God, and will my own children be silent?!" All creation is alive with the glory of God. The divine presence is constantly being revealed to us through the fabric of creation, how can we not give voice and sing? Joy to the world!

A joy-filled noise

Lost somewhere in the memories of my childhood, after I memorized the 23rd Psalm, at Sunday School or Vacation Bible School, I committed to memory the words of Psalm 100. I expect that every Sunday they are used in some congregation as their opening call to worship, for that is what it is: An invitation to praise God, to worship God, to make joy filled noise. Psalm 100 has been set to music in the classic hymn appropriately called "Old One Hundredth," "All people that on earth do dwell."

For most of its history, Israel was a small, out-of-the-way country. It was a nation of little note, most of the time ruled by its more powerful neighbors. In this Psalm, Israel super sizes itself, calling all the nations to worship God, all the people to praise God, the whole earth to make a joyful noise. And worship is joyful, exuberant, delighting in the divine. God is good and God is creator, therefore, creation is good. God is compassionate and comforts us. We praise God, glorify God, give thanks to God, and sing joyfully.

I remember hearing from missionaries in Africa that the highlight of public worship in most African churches was always the offering. Instead of passing the plates, people joined in a parade, bringing their gifts to the altar, thrilled with the opportunity to give thanks to God, to return some small portion of all that God blessed them with. What a contrast to most of our middle class white American congregations, where we try to sneak past the offering and be as unobtrusive as possible. We need to make a joyful noise!

Bless the Lord, O my Soul!

Here again is a Psalm that is part of my daily diet. Psalm 103 celebrates God's presence and goodness, a Psalm that praises God for being God. The first of five verses are oft repeated. The Psalm as a whole is one I would read at every funeral or memorial service in walking to the gravesite, leading coffin and mourners. Even in death, we celebrate the goodness of God, we recall our many blessings, and we give thanks for what is ours while we have it.

"Bless the Lord, O my soul, and all that is within me, bless God's holy name. Bless the Lord, O my soul, do not forget God's benefits, who forgives your iniquity, who heals your disease, who redeems your life, who crowns you with steadfast love and mercy, who satisfies you with good as long as you live, who renews your youth like the eagle's." (v. 1-5)

I would repeat these words between rooms at the hospital or between homes during visitation. Bless the Lord, O my soul! The rest of the Psalm recalls God's mercy and goodness, God's grace and love. God treats us better than we deserve and loves us more than we can know. We are designed to be temporary; death is part of the plan. But God's steadfast love endures forever. Psalm 103 recalls incidents and events with which we can identify. It is personal as well as transcendent. It celebrates both our humanity and God's holiness, God's otherness. We have a place in God's creation, a role to play in the divine drama. It is ours, God's gift to us. But we are not God. We play our part and then move on, as a divine drama continues.

Now retired, I joke that the only thing I have to do is ensure Becki's happiness, and she is happy to see me leave the house and do other things. When I was 10 years old I decided I wanted to have a doctorate and be a published author. Nerdy goals for a 10-year-old! I have accomplished that. I have had my career and raised my kids. They now raise kids of their own and have their own careers and lives before them. So I have done my job. Yet each day is a blessing and a gift, a sacred renewal. Each day is an opportunity to experience the divine, to discover the eternal in our everyday moments, the extraordinary in the ordinary. Each day is another refrain in that song of praise, "bless the Lord, O my soul, everything that is within me, bless God's holy name!"

A Never-Ending Story

Psalms 103, 104 and 105 go together like a poetic triptych. Psalm 103 is personal praise of God for all God's goodness in one's life. Psalm 104 recalls God's care in all creation. Psalm 105 recites God's mighty acts in the history of God's chosen people Israel.

In high school, my biology teacher challenged me to write my term paper on what the Bible says about creation and evolution. I naively agreed. When I got home, I asked Dad what the Bible says about creation. His response surprised me, "Which place?" he asked. I thought there was only one creation story, in Genesis chapters one and two. He said no, they were actually two different creation accounts, and the Bible contains several others, among them Psalm 8 and Psalm 104. Psalm 104 celebrates God's power and glory revealed through God's act of creation and ongoing support of it. All creation is a revealing of God. The psalm ends in worship, praising and glorifying God. I celebrate creation as God's revelation in *Creation in Contemporary Experience*.

Psalm 105 reminds us of the covenant God established with Israel as God's chosen people, God's favored nation. It recites their history: their slavery in Egypt, the plagues that won their freedom, the signs and wonders Moses wrought in the wilderness, and a call for Israel to keep the laws that God commands. Psalm 106 continues as a litany confessing Israel's sins throughout their history, how they have failed to keep those commands, and asks God to have pity on God's people and save them in spite of themselves. Even the best of us fail at times; in the end, we are all saved by grace.

Question for Reflection

Sit with pen and paper. Consider all the ways God has blessed your life, all the many blessings that are part of your life. List them, and let them remind you of still more blessings. Read through the list and let these blessings also bless you.

Question for Discussion

Psalms 103 talks about God with us personally. Psalm 104 shares abut God in creation and Psalm 105 about God in human history. Consider ways God may have been experienced by members of the group personally, through encounters in nature or the actions of others.

Question for Action

The Psalms remind us over and again that this is God's world and we are God's appointed caretakers. Take some time this week to clean some public space, maybe as a group.

Closing Prayer

Bless the Lord, bless God's holy name! With thoughts and prayers, with song and praise, with action and deed, with lives of faithful wit-

ness and steadfast service. In all we do, think, say and feel, we bless you, God, and glorify your holy name. May your presence shine through our lives so that others may see you through the light of our witness. Amen.

Psalms 115 – 150

"O Lord, you have searched me and known me, you are intimate in all my ways. Such knowledge is too great for me; I cannot comprehend it." Psalm 139:1,6

Not to us

"Not to us, O Lord, not ever to us. But to your name be glory, to your name be praise. For your steadfast love is great toward us and your abiding faithfulness endures forever." Psalm 115:1

Years ago I went to a concert by the Imperials, a contemporary Christian music band. One of the songs in their repertoire is the sung version of this verse; it really struck a chord with me. "Not to us O Lord, not ever to us. But to your name be glory, to your name be praise. For your steadfast love is great toward us and your abiding faithfulness endures forever."

Our faith can never be about ourselves, we are not the point, regardless of who that "we" might be. Our faith is about God, the Divine that is over and under and before and behind and within all that we do, think, say or feel, all that we are. In over 30 years of preaching, I frequently said that nobody comes to church to hear me preach or hear what I have to say. They come to hear what God has to say, to experience the presence of the living God. Nobody is saved in the name of Dave, not even Dave. Like the verses of Samuel Wesley from Psalms 4 and 5, this is a verse that I sing and say and pray on a regular ongoing basis.

Consistent with the whole of scripture, the text of the Psalm is essentially a rebuttal against atheism or polytheism. The Bible does in places describe our God as one among other gods, as the one we worship and the supreme deity. This is called henotheism, worshiping one god among many. Some have described an evolving understanding of God in the Bible, from a tribal deity for the Hebrews, to one among many, to the supreme being, to the one universal and cosmic divine. Where is our God? Our God does whatever God wants, whatever God pleases to do. Their images are mere idols we can have confidence in our God, for our God blesses us helps us protects us and is mindful of us God will give us increase in possessions and in posterity. The dead do not praise God; not dead people or dead images or dead ideas, but we will bless God forever.

The point is never about us. Our faith is not about us, our worship is not about us, our church is not about us, our lives are not about us. Our lives belong to our God. Our church is the flesh and blood incarnation of the body of Christ. Our worship focuses on the divine presence of the living God.

Again, the psalmist celebrates the all-mighty power of the living God, the unsearchable wisdom of God, the omnipresence of the divine, and most of all, most of all, God's steadfast love of us and God's abiding faithfulness.

Praise the Lord!

Psalm 117 is one I grew up with as a table grace. At home, breakfast and lunch might be informal, but we usually had dinner together as a family, and always began with table grace. There were a few that mom and dad would repeat on a regular basis, expecting that we kids would pick them up almost by osmosis. This plan certainly worked with Psalm 117. It is short and wonderfully to the point, making it a perfect dinner time prayer for five hungry children. I used the same strategy with my sons. My oldest son, Jason, took to it immediately. He recited the Psalm as an evangelist might.

When driving to visit with family, I would frequently take little side trips to see other churches. I would look at their architecture and location and see how they presented themselves to the public, what kind of message did their physical presence make to the community they served. Jason would be in the back seat, in his car seat, taking it all in. When we had checked it out and satisfied our curiosity, as we were pulling away, Jason would exclaim" praise the Lord!" With his arms high over his head giving God the glory.

I remember our reciting Psalm 117 at the dinner table, and Jason standing on his chair, arms raised high above his head, as he recited the entire Psalm, "praise the Lord all you people! Praise God all you nations! God's steadfast love is great toward us, and the strength of the Lord endures forever. Praise the Lord!" Then he was ready for his supper. Having fed his soul, he is ready to feed his stomach.

The law is our life

Psalm 119 is easily the longest psalm in the Bible, at 176 verses. It is composed as an acrostic, with a stanza of eight verses for each of the twenty-two letters of the Hebrew alphabet. It is a meditation and a teaching on the Law of God as the way of life.

We tend to think of laws as lists of "thou shalt nots," defining and confining our liberties. Here are things we are not supposed to do, and if we do them, there will be consequences we don't like. We get speeding tickets and arrest warrants. A list of 176 things we are not to do seems extreme!

Augustine said "Love God and do as you will."[6] The oath of Hippocrates was "Do no harm." Jesus summarized the law and the prophets with two rules: love God and love your neighbor. These seem simpler and more positive. But it is not the purpose of Psalm 119 to beat us up with rules and regulations. Instead, it is a devotional reflection praising God for the life-giving gift of the divine law. It is even affectionate in its approach. It extols God for the gift of the law and encourages us to live by this law. Several different words are used to describe the law, signifying the intimate and dynamic relationship the author has with it. The law of God is the yearning, longing, desiring of God for us; it is how God expresses God's love and desire for us. This may be summarized by the words of verse 105, often set to music, "Thy word is a lamp unto my feet and a light upon my path."

---

6   Augustine of Hippo: *Seventh Homily on First John.*

Next year, Jerusalem!

As mentioned earlier, there are eighteen imprecatory psalms, psalms that express our anger, ask for vengeance, and are honest about our dark side, challenging us to be just as honest with God as these psalms are. It is only fair, then, to also recognize our bright side. There is a group of psalms, from 120 through 134, that are identified as "Songs of Ascent." They are happy and hopeful, even cheerful, celebrating our approach to the divine. Three are identified with David, one with Solomon, the others anonymous, but their authorship is not the point; their intended use is more relevant.

Judaism celebrates three annual pilgrimage feasts: Passover, Pentecost, and Tabernacles. They are expected to celebrate these holy days in Jerusalem, their holy city (and a holy city for three world religions: Judaism, Christianity, and Islam). You are expected to make this pilgrimage if at all possible. Especially in ancient times, this imposed considerable hardship and was not always possible. Being able to make the pilgrimage was a cause for celebration. Each of the world's religions encourages pilgrimage: a pilgrimage is an outer journey with an inner purpose; see my *Life as Pilgrimage: A View from Celtic Spirituality.*[7] These fifteen psalms, "Songs of Ascent," would be recited, even sung, as pilgrims approached their destination of Jerusalem. The Holy City was conquered by King David to be his capital and hailed as the City of God, that God would bless and shield, through all history. There would be much rejoicing in its approach. There is also a theory that one of these psalms would be recited for each of the fifteen steps as one entered the temple.

If we can confess our anger in the imprecatory psalms and admit our dark side, certainly we can cherish any experience of holy joy and celebrate our life as a spiritual pilgrimage. The order for the annual Passover meal, the holiest event of the year, ends with an aspiration, a hope more than a promise, "Next year, in Jerusalem!"

---

7   David Moffatt-Moore: *Life as Pilgrimage: A View from Celtic Spirituality.* Energion Publications, 2nd Edition, 2013.

Out of the depths

I first encountered Psalm 130 as I prepared to do my first funeral. The first time we do anything there is an element of discomfort in the unfamiliarity of the task. How much more is this true for a funeral. We do not like facing the reality of our own mortality. We have created an industry to protect us from dealing with the reality of our demise. I read this Psalm and found it to be dark, heavy. I thought about omitting it from the funeral service, but I was new and thought that perhaps the first time I should follow the directions, so I kept it in. After the service members of the family volunteered how much they appreciated these words, how it gave voice to the aching in their hearts. "Out of the depths I cry to you O Lord. Lord, hear my voice!"

There are dark nights when all we can do is wait silently and hope, when all we can do is remember God's goodness in the past and hold on for God's goodness to again be revealed. This is a part of the human condition, we all have our highs and our lows. And we need words that give voice to our emotions. We long for the Lord, and find our hope in God's words and in God's Word.

A humble heart

Psalm 131 is one that I literally tripped over. I was having a mood, a bit of a tiff. I was looking for some ammunition that I could fire back with, Scripture I could use as a sword, that would make me right. I was not looking for words of calmness and quiet trust. I was not looking for it, but it certainly was what I needed.

> "O Lord, my heart is not haughty, my eyes are not raised up, I do not fill myself with things too great and marvelous for me to understand. I have calmed my soul and quieted myself, like a weaned child in its mother's arms, like a weaned child is my soul within me. O Israel, hope in the Lord, from this time forth and forevermore!"

I have two doctorates, seven books published, over 30 years of experience as a pastor, over a decade as an investment advisor and manager. I have taught a variety of subjects at a variety of colleges. I have demonstrated excellence in a number of fields. It is easy for my heart to be haughty and my eyes to be raised up, to fill my mind with great and marvelous things. But none of this really matters, none of it is the point, none of it is of any lasting importance. The only thing that really matters is to be that weaned child in God's loving arms.

We're used to masculine images of the divine, God as king and father. God as "he." The God I know is not some big guy in the sky. God is no more male than God is rock or fortress. God is not a being, but rather beingness itself. That which is, present past or future, tangible and intangible, physically, spiritually, or energetically.

The Bible does have feminine images of the divine, and they are quite powerful also. God is the mother bear protecting her young. God is the mother eagle teaching her young to fly. God is the mother hen gathering her chicks about her. The act of creation is profoundly feminine. Only women know what it is like to form an entirely new being from the stuff of their own being. And this Psalm, for God is a loving mother, nursing her young. Oh to be that infant! Wrapped in the arms of divine love and nursing on the divine presence! May I have that simplicity, that clarity, that intimacy. Meister Eckhardt, a medieval mystic, describes God as lying in bed, continually giving birth to creation.

God's steadfast love endures forever!

When I first entered the ministry in my 20s, there were times I thought perhaps I was borderline manic-depressive, I had such extreme highs and lows. I reveled in the highs and worked to find ways to climb out of the depths of those lows. I think congregations can go through emotional swings as well, between the highs and lows of life. There have been times when I have used Psalm 136 as a ladder out of the depths. In this Psalm we repeat 26 times that God's steadfast love endures forever. When we are vain and focused on ourselves, God's steadfast love endures forever, and remember that it is not about us and our glory. When you are having a hard time and were disappointed in ourselves are down on ourselves, God's steadfast love endures forever. In good times and bad, in celebration and defeat, in the mundane repetition of our everyday ordinariness, God's steadfast love endures forever! Just to be sure that we get the point, we repeat this truth 26 times!

Divine intimacy

I was privileged to be a member of the first class of the Academy of Spiritual Formation, sponsored by the Upper Room in Nashville Tennessee. This is an intensive two-year program in spirituality. My spiritual director at one point encouraged me to not just read but to pray Psalm 139 every day for 30 days and see the effect this discipline would have on me. I was amazed.

The Psalm describes a very intimate, trusting relationship with a God who is at once overwhelmingly wondrous, unlimited in power, unbounded in love, and intimately present. I invite you, as part of your exploration of the Psalms, to follow the same experiment. Let the words of the song be planted as spiritual seeds your soul. Read the words of Psalm 139 through slowly, thoughtfully, prayerfully. Let them take root and grow in your heart, bear fruit in your life. Pray the psalm. Let it become part of you. Let it nurture your spirit.

The psalmist knows their position before the divine. The psalmist is humble, trusting, confident, and filled with wonder, a good way to stand before the divine presence. This is a stance we see throughout the Psalms. This is a stance the psalmist encourages us to take.

God is above and beyond anything we can think, feel, or imagine. God knows us better than we know ourselves, and his love for us is greater then we can love ourselves. Great is the Lord, and greatly to be praised!

Church and state

We have much public discourse swirling about concerning the relationship between church and state and the influence private faith may have over public politics. The First Amendment to our Constitution stipulates "Congress shall make no law respecting the establishment or prohibiting the free exercise of religion." Yet we expect our Presidents to be people of faith, preferably members in good standing, who take their oath for office upon some sacred Scripture. Our faith leaders often encourage us to vote on matters of politics according to some persuasion of faith.

Thomas Jefferson, author of our Declaration of Independence, who served as Secretary of State, Vice-President and President, was a deist and proponent of natural religion. Not believing in miracles, he excised Jesus' miracles from his New Testament. Nonetheless, he offered up Psalm 148 as the supreme example and evidence for the God of nature and creation to which he could espouse. Psalm 148 calls on all creation to glorify God: in, with, through and for creation, God is to be praised!

Late in life, in his correspondence with John Adams, Jefferson offered up this Psalm as proof and pattern for his personal faith.

The union that Jefferson helped establish was rocked to its core by the Civil War, presided over by Abraham Lincoln and precipitated by his election. Raised a Baptist, Lincoln was quiet about his personal faith but well versed in the Scriptures. He regarded his second inaugural speech as his greatest speech. Less well known than his Gettysburg Address, it is really a sermon to the nation. Previous inaugural speeches had referred euphemistically to God; in this speech, Lincoln was explicit and honest about the work that was needed to heal the nation. It contains barely 700 words, 500 of which are one syllable. God is mentioned fourteen times, Scripture is quoted five times and prayer is invoked four times.

He quotes from Matthew 7:1 and 18:7 and James 1:27 in the New Testament. His Old Testament references are both from the Psalms. Psalm 19:9, "The fear of the Lord is pure, enduring forever; the judgments of the Lord are true, righteous altogether." And appropriate for the healing of the nation, from Psalm 147:3, God heals the brokenhearted and binds up their wounds."

From two of our greatest presidents, half of Mt. Rushmore, we have public attestation and personal confession of the influence of and formation offered by this collection of poems and prayers in the Psalms.

Praise the Lord!

The last several Psalms that close out the book are all psalms of praise. It is a good way to end the list of prayers, complaints, confessions, and invocations for revenge. For all their honest humanity, the Psalms remember that God is good, that creation is good, that life is good and we have much to be thankful for.

I had the blessing of serving a church that had paid off their mortgage, after much work and effort and sacrifice, after fundraising dinners and sales, after fish fries and bake sales. We were relieved and joyous and grateful. We decided to burn the mortgage as part of our Sunday morning worship service. I encouraged people to bring noisemakers. I admit to being a bit surprised when one member showed up with a cannon. It had a charge, but no cannonball. We set a match to the now-canceled mortgage, shouted out the text of the 150th Psalm, and then let loose with the noisemakers, cannon and all. Imagine the ruckus!

> "Praise the Lord! Praise God in the sanctuary! Praise God in the highest heavens! Praise God in all creation! Praise God for mighty deeds! Praise God for outstanding greatness! Praise God with trumpet, with harp and a lyre, with tambourine and dancing, with strings and pipe. Praise God with cymbals, with loud cymbals, with loud clashing cymbals! Let everything that has breath praise the Lord!"

God is good, all the time. All the time, God is good. How can we not rejoice, give thanks, and offer praise! Let the wild ruckus begin!

Question for Reflection

What prayers did you grow up repeating and remembering? How have they sustained you along the way?

Question for Discussion

How are we living our lives so that they point to God? How are we living proofs of God's presence?

Question for Action

Who in your life is going through a difficult time? How can you offer them comfort and encouragement? Then do so!

Closing Prayer

Praise the Lord, sun and moon! Praise the Lord, day and night! Praise the Lord seed-time and harvest! Praise the Lord trees and flowers, rocks and hills, birds and fish! May all creation praise the Lord! May we, God's creatures and children, praise the Lord with humble grateful hearts. Praise the Lord! Amen.

Blessings

We have concluded a study, opening the scriptures to us and us to the scriptures. Hebrews 4:12 reminds us "The word of God is living and active, sharper than any two-edged sword, dividing soul and spirit like joints and marrow and able to discern the desires of our hearts." Hopefully, you have experienced some of this. Hopefully, you have found yourself read by the scriptures as you read them. I have long felt that the scriptures serve as a window into our own true selves as much as they are a window to God's will.

This has been intended as a devotional study rather than an academic one. As the prayer book and songbook of the Bible, the rightful place of the Psalms is as devotional literature. They are not designed to stimulate theological discussions or doctrinal debates. It is not enough to read with our heads, we must also read with our hearts. Intellectual insight is good; spiritual insight is better. They are meant to move us to pray or motivate us to sing, to inspire rather than inform. They help us pray when our hearts can't find the words. Unlike most of the Bible, the Psalms are not meant to be read through in their entirety in one sitting. You can read the gospels in one sitting and it would be good to do so. Reading the Psalms through in one sitting would be tiresome for the reader and not very productive. Rather, the Psalms are to be read individually. Read it, ponder it, reflect on it. Let it settle. Ruminate on the word of the Psalms.

You have read psalms, prayed psalms and sung psalms. You have rejoiced in psalms of thanksgiving, ached in psalms of abandonment and distress, perhaps screamed in the imprecatory psalms, wept in psalms of sorrow, grieved in psalms of confession, and stood in awe and wonder in psalms of adoration. Hopefully, it has been an emotional experience as much as an intellectual one.

While my sister Susan kept vigil over her distressed husband Michael. When I struggled with my own sense of call to the ministry, seeking discernment or insight or at least respite. The Psalms are like the old hallway boxes containing fire hose: "in emergency, break glass!" I hope this study has done that. I hope the study has been devotional. I hope you have been able to participate not only with a group of fellow pilgrims in this Participatory Bible Study, but that you have been able to participate mind, body, and soul, with all the fullness of your being. I hope you have a better familiarity with and understanding of the Psalms, but more importantly, I hope they have become more a part of your daily life, indeed, your every breath.

I can imagine King David as a boy, sitting alone on a hilltop watching over his flock, playing his harp in the halls of the king or hiding from King Saul's guards in a cave. I imagine David, inspired to sing and pray. There have been moments of inspiration in my life when I felt moved to write poetry or even a sermon. I hope this study has at some point opened your heart to the divine presence that is always with us: within and around, above and beneath, before and behind – always.

In writing this book, I have used as resources chiefly the books on the Psalms I inherited from Dad when he retired and the few devotional treatments on the Psalms I have purchased. It has been a time for me to connect with my father through shared texts.

My father started his seminary education at Yale Divinity School, where his faculty advisor was the Rev. Dr. George Dahl. Dr. Dahl was the translator of the Psalms for the Revised Standard Version of the Bible, the Old Testament of which was published in 1952. Dad also took the course on the Psalms that Dr. Dahl led. Dad described him as a challenging instructor and a wise counselor. His influence strengthened Dad's fondness for the Psalms. If I have followed in his footsteps, I have done well.

This book is dedicated to my mother, Ruth Frances Elliott Moore. She grew up with four sisters on a farm outside of Wabash, Indiana. Early in her life, she felt God's call, but being a woman, she was not encouraged to follow it. After college, she attended Scarritt School for Women in Nashville, that trained women to be lay workers in churches. She worked at a church with children and youth and visitation, doing what an Associate Pastor might do. She married Dad; in part I think that since she couldn't be a pastor, she would marry one. Then the bishop warned his pastors to keep their wives out of church affairs. So we five siblings became Mom's congregation. Many times she encouraged me with daring stories about brave missionaries. I hope this collection communicates some of the passion she felt and some of the disappointment in the delay and deferment from the God whom we adore.

My two greatest influences in seminary were my New Testament professors: Dr. Richard Stegner at Garrett Evangelical Theological Seminary at Northwestern University and Dr. Irv Batdorf at United Theological Seminary at Dayton, Ohio. They taught me to use my head in studying the scripture, to use historical and literary criticism and apply my best reasoning. They also taught me that reason alone is never enough, that loving God required heart and guts as well, that emotion was as much a part of study as intellect. As Jesus recited the Shema of Deuteronomy 6:4-5 as the greatest commandment, "Love the Lord your God with all your heart and soul and mind and might." As Hebrews warns (4:12) "the word of God is alive and active, sharper than any two edged sword, piercing soul and spirit, separating joints and marrow, knowing our thoughts and hidden intentions."

Who have been most influential in your spiritual pilgrimage? How have they served to help shape your faith? How is their influence evident in your daily life?

My Ph.D. is in Celtic Spirituality. I remember that Irish mother, scolding her children for neglecting their prayers: "The sun in the sky glows for the love of God, the clouds in the sky float for the love of God, the birds of the air fly for the love of God, the fish of the sea swim for the love of God, the sheep bleat and the cattle mew for the love of God, the trees blossom and the flowers bloom for the love of God. And will my own children be silent?" I remember St. Patrick's Breastplate: "Christ be with me, Christ before me, Christ behind me, Christ within me, Christ around me,

Christ beneath me, Christ above me, Christ on my right, Christ on my left, Christ when I lie down, Christ when I sit, Christ when I arise, Christ in the heart of everyone who thinks of me, Christ in the mouth of everyone who speaks of me, Christ in every eye that sees me, Christ in every ear that hears me."

How have you experienced God through this study, both in personal preparation and in group sharing? What impact has it had that might be long term? What difference has it made?

I invite you to write your own psalm. You have spent the last several weeks studying them, living with them, experiencing them. You've gotten used to their sense and flow. I invite you to sit at a table with pen and paper. Take a few long, slow, deep breaths. Wait and listen. Then take up your pen and write. Let the words flow, not from your head but from your heart. Let your heart speak to God's heart and let God's heart reply in return, all through the ink you place on that paper. Let it be as a living document. Read it and see what it says to you, as your heart cries out.

I hope this study has been for you a time of renewal and growth, that you are more aware of the divine presence within and around you and that others may see that presence more fully through your life. May Christ be with you, may the love of God fill you, and may your life be a hymn and a prayer, a psalm, as your heart cries out!

Question for Reflection

What difference, if any, has this study made in your life?

Question for Discussion

What have been your highs and lows during this study? What answers have you found and what questions have been raised?

Question for Action

What happens next? Is there another topic you wish to explore? Where is God leading you?

Closing Prayer

God, you have blessed us and guided us through this time of study and fellowship. We thank you for your presence, your guidance and the growth you have brought to us. May our lives continue to be filled with prayer and praise. May our hearts constantly cry out for your presence in our lives. Amen.

A SUPERNUMERARY PSALM

Psalm 151 has only fairly recently been known in Western circles. It is recognized in the Orthodox tradition and known in Jewish circles, though it is not in the usual count. It is intended to be David's personal recollections after fighting and killing Goliath.

"I was small among my brothers, the youngest of my father's sons. I was only a shepherd of my father's sheep.

My hands made for music; my fingers to play the harp.

Who will tell my Lord? The Lord personally hears me.

The Lord sent a messenger, and took me away from my father's sheep, anointing my head with oil.

My brothers were handsome, tall and strong, but the Lord did not take any pleasure in them.

I went out to meet the Philistine, who cursed and shamed us by his idols.

But I took his own sword out of its sheath and cut off his head. So I removed the shame from all of Israel."

It is nothing profound or earth-shattering, nothing that will challenge any existing understanding of the Psalms in particular or faith in general. It does remind us of David's encounter with Samuel as well as Goliath, how David was the youngest and smallest, and that God looks not at the appearance but at the heart, the essence of a person, and that God is directly involved in the seeming ordinariness of our daily lives.

READING LIST

Bonhoeffer, Dietrich. *Psalms: The Prayer Book of the Bible*. Augsburg Press. Minneapolis. 1974.

Brueggemann, Walter. *The Message of the Psalms*. Augsburg Publishing. Minneapolis. 1984.

Futato, Mark D. *Interpreting the Psalms: An Exegetical Handbook*. Kregel Academic. Grand Rapids. 2007

Hawkins, Thomas R. *The Unsuspected Power of the Psalms*. The Upper Room. Nashville. 1985

Laymon, Charles M., ed. *The Interpreter's One-Volume Commentary on the Bible*. Abingdon Press. Nashville. 1971

Leslie, Elmer A. *The Psalms*. Abingdon Press. Nashville. 1949

Lewis, C.S. *Reflections on the Psalms*. Harcourt, Brace. New York. 1958.

Macbeath, John. *A Wayfarer's Psalter*. Marshall, Morgan and Scott. London. 1944.

Rhodes, A. B. *Psalms*. SCM Press. London. 1960.

Weiser, Artur. *The Psalms*. Westminster Press. Philadelphia. 1962.

Wenham, Gordon J. *Psalms as Torah: Reading Biblical Song Ethically*. Baker Academic. Ada, MI 2012

CPSIA information can be obtained
at www.ICGtesting.com
Printed in the USA
JSHW010224121219
2896JS00003B/30